Henry VIII and His Court

HENRY VIII
From the Portrait by Holbein, at Warwick Castle

HENRY VIII
AND HIS COURT

BY

HERBERT BEERBOHM TREE

WITH FOUR FULL-PAGE PLATES

SIXTH EDITION

FOLCROFT LIBRARY EDITIONS / 1977

HENRY VIII
AND HIS COURT

BY

HERBERT BEERBOHM TREE

WITH FOUR FULL-PAGE PLATES

SIXTH EDITION

CASSELL AND COMPANY, LTD.
London, New York, Toronto and Melbourne
1911

INTRODUCTORY

IN these notes, written as a holiday task, it is not intended to give an exhaustive record of the events of Henry's reign; but rather to offer an impression of the more prominent personages in Shakespeare's play; and perhaps to aid the playgoer in a fuller appreciation of the conditions which governed their actions.

Marienbad, 1930

CONTENTS

LIST OF PLATES

KING HENRY VIII

KING HENRY VIII

His Character

HOLBEIN has drawn the character and written
the history of Henry on the canvas of his
great picture. Masterful, cruel, crafty, merci-
less, courageous, sensual, through-seeing, hu-
morous, mean, matter of fact, worldly-wise,
and of indomitable will, Henry the Eighth
is perhaps the most outstanding figure in
English history. The reason is not far to
seek. The genial adventurer with sporting
tendencies and large-hearted proclivities is
always popular with the mob, and " Bluff
King Hal," as ne was called, was of the
eternal type adored by the people. He had
a certain outward and inward affinity with
Nero. Like Nero, he was corpulent; like
Nero, he was red-haired; like Nero, he sang
and poetised; like Nero, he was a lover of
horsemanship, a master of the arts and the
slave of his passions. If his private vices were
great, his public virtues were no less considerable. He had the ineffable quality called

charm, and the appearance of good-nature which captivated all who came within the orbit of his radiant personality. He was the "*beau garçon*," endearing himself to all women by his compelling and conquering manhood. Henry was every inch a man, but he was no gentleman. He chucked even Justice under the chin, and Justice winked her blind eye.

It is extraordinary that in spite of his brutality, both Katharine and Anne Boleyn spoke of him as a model of kindness. This cannot be accounted for alone by that divinity which doth hedge a king.

There is, above all, in the face of Henry, as depicted by Holbein, that look of impenetrable mystery which was the background of his character. Many royal men have this strange quality ; with some it is inborn, with others it is assumed. Of Henry, Cavendish,* a contemporary, records the following saying : " Three may keep counsel, if two be away ; and if I thought my cap knew my counsel,

---

* Cavendish was Wolsey's faithful secretary, and after his fall wrote the interesting " Life of Wolsey," one of the manuscript copies of which evidently fell into Shakespeare's hands before he wrote *Henry VIII.*

I would throw it in the fire and burn
it." Referring to this passage, Brewer says,
" Never had the King spoke a truer word or
described himself more accurately. Few
would have thought that, under so careless
and splendid an exterior—the very ideal of
bluff, open-hearted good humour and frankness—there lay a watchful and secret mind
that marked what was going on without
seeming to mark it ; kept its own counsel
until it was time to strike, and then struck
as suddenly and remorselessly as a, beast of
prey. It was strange to witness so much
subtlety combined with so much strength."

There was something baffling and terrify-
ing in the mysterious bonhomie of the King.
In spite of Cæsar's dictum, it is the fat enemy
who is to be feared ; a thin villain is more
easily seen through.

His Ancestry

Henry's antecedents were far from glorious.
The Tudors were a Welsh family of somewhat
humble stock. Henry VII.'s great-grand-
father was butler or steward to the Bishop
of Bangor, whose son, Owen Tudor, coming

to London, obtained a clerkship of the
Wardrobe to Henry V.'s Queen, Catherine of
France. Within a few years of Henry's
death, the widowed Queen and her clerk of
the wardrobe were secretly living together as
man and wife. The two sons of this mor-
ganatic match, Edmund and Jasper, were
favoured by their half brother, Henry VI.
Edmund, the elder, was knighted, and then
made Earl of Richmond. In 1453 he was
formally declared legitimate, and enrolled a
member of the King's Council. Two years
later he married the Lady Margaret Beaufort,
a descendant of Edward III. It was this
union between Edmund Tudor and Margaret
Beaufort which gave Henry VII. his claim
by descent to the English throne.

The popularity of the Tudors was, no
doubt, enhanced by the fact that with their
line, kings of decisively English blood, for the
first time since the Norman Conquest, sat on
the English throne.

His Early Days

When Henry VIII. ascended the throne in
1509, England regarded him with almost

universal loyalty. The memory of the long years of the Wars of the Roses and the wars of the Pretenders during the reign of his father, were fresh in the people's mind. No other than he could have attained to the throne without civil war.

Within two months he married Katharine of Aragon, his brother's widow, and a few days afterwards the King and Queen were crowned with great splendour in Westminster Abbey. He was still in his eighteenth year, of fine physical development, but of no special mental precocity. For the first five years of his reign, he was influenced by his Council, and especially by his father-in-law, Ferdinand the Catholic, giving little indication of the later mental vigour and power of initiation which made his reign so memorable in English annals.

The political situation in Europe was a difficult one for Henry to deal with. France and Spain were the rivals for Imperial dominion. England was in danger of falling between two stools, such was the eagerness of each that the other should not support her. Henry, through his marriage with

Katharine, began by being allied to Spain, and this alliance involved England in the costly burden of war. Henry's resentment at the empty result of this warfare, broke the Spanish alliance. Wolsey's aim was to keep the country out of wars, and a long period of peace raised England to the position of arbiter of Europe in the balanced contest between France and Spain.

The Field of the Cloth of Gold

It was in connection with the meetings and intrigues now with one power, now with the other, that the famous meeting with the French King at Guisnes, known as " the Field of the Cloth of Gold," was held in 1520.

That the destinies of kingdoms sometimes hang on trifles is curiously exemplified by a singular incident which preceded the famous meeting. Francis I. prided himself on his beard. As a proof of his desire for the meeting with Francis, and out of compliment to the French King, Henry announced his resolve to wear his beard uncut until the meeting took place. But he reckoned without

his wife. Some weeks before the meeting
Louise of Savoy, the Queen-Mother of France,
taxed Boleyn, the English Ambassador, with
a report that Henry had put off his beard.
" I said," writes Boleyn, " that, as I suppose,
it hath been by the Queen's desire, for I told
my lady that I have hereafore known when
the King's grace hath worn long his beard,
that the Queen hath daily made him great
instance, and desired him to put it off for
her sake." This incident caused some resentment on the part of the French King, who
was only pacified by Henry's tact.

So small a matter might have proved a
casus belli.

The meeting was held amidst scenes of
unparalleled splendour. The temporary palace
erected for the occasion was so magnificent
that a chronicler tells us it might have been
the work of Leonardo da Vinci. Henry " the
goodliest prince that ever reigned over the
realm of England," is described as " *honnête,
hault et droit,* in manner gentle and gracious,
rather fat, with a red beard, large enough,
and very becoming."

On this occasion Wolsey was accompanied

by two hundred gentlemen clad in crimson velvet, and had a body-guard of two hundred archers. He was clothed in crimson satin from head to foot, his mule was covered with crimson velvet, and her trappings were all of gold.

There were jousts and many entertainments and rejoicings, many kissings of Royal cheeks, but the Sovereigns hated each other cordially. While they were kissing they were plotting against each other. A more unedifying page of history has not been written. Appalling, indeed, are the shifts and intrigues which go to make up the records of the time.

The rulers of Europe were playing a game of cards, in which all the players were in collusion with, and all cheating each other. Temporizing and intriguing, Henry met the Spanish monarch immediately before and immediately after his meeting with the French King. Within a few months, France and Spain were again at war, and England, in a fruitless and costly struggle, fought on the side of Spain.

It was the divorce from Katharine of Aragon and its momentous consequences, which finally put an end to the alliance with Spain, and to the struggle with France succeeded a long struggle with Spain, which culminated in the great event of The Armada in the reign of Henry's daughter, Elizabeth.

However, in these pages it is not proposed to enlarge upon the political aspect of the times, but rather to deal with the dramatic and domestic side of Henry's being. In the play of *Henry VIII.*, the author or authors (for to another than Shakespeare is ascribed a portion of the drama), have given us as impartial a view of his character as a due regard for truth on the one hand, and a respect for the scaffold on the other, permitted.

His Aspirations

There can be no doubt that when Henry ascended the throne, he had a sincere wish to serve God and uphold the right.

In his early years he was really devout and generous in almsgiving. Erasmus affirmed that his Court was an example to all Christendom for learning and piety. To the Pope he paid deference as to the representative of God.

With youthful enthusiasm, the young King,

looking round and seeing corruption on every side, said to Giustinian, the Venetian ambassador : " Nor do I see any faith in the world save in me, and therefore God Almighty, who knows this, prosper my affairs."

In Henry's early reign, England was trusted more than any country to keep faith in her alliances. At a time when all was perfidy and treachery, promises and alliances were made only to be broken when self-interest prompted. History, like Nature itself, is ruled by brutal laws, and to play the round game of politics with single-handed honesty would be to lose at every turn. Henry was born into an inheritance of blood and blackmail. Corruption has its vested interests. It is useless to attempt to stem the recurrent tide of corruption by sprinkling the waves with holy water.

Then religion was a part of men's daily lives, but the principles of Christianity were set at naught at the first bidding of expediency.

Men murdered to live—the axe and the sword were the final Court of Appeal. Nor does the old order change appreciably in the course of a few hundred years. In international politics, as in public life, when self-interest steps in, Christianity goes to the wall.

To-day we grind our axe with a difference. A more subtle process of dealing with our rivals obtains. To-day the pen is mightier than the sword, the stylograph is more deadly than the stiletto. The bravo still plies his trade. He no longer takes life, but character. To intrigue, to combine against those outside the ring is often the swiftest way to fortune. By such combination do weaker particles make themselves strong. To " play the game " is necessary to progress. The world was not made for poets and idealists. To quote an anonymous modern writer :

" ' Act well your part, there all the honour lies ' ;
Stoop to expediency and honour dies.
Many there are that in the race for fame,
Lose the great cause to win the little game,
Who pandering to the town's decadent taste,
Barter the precious pearl for gawdy paste,
And leave upon the virgin page of Time
The venom'd trail of iridescent slime."

Henry's eyes soon opened. His character, like his body, underwent a gradual process of expansion.

His Pastimes

Soon the lighter side of kingship was not disdained. One authority wrote in 1515 : " He is a youngling, cares for nothing but girls and hunting." He was an inveterate gambler, and turned the sport of hunting into a martyrdom, rising at four or five in the morning, and hunting till nine or ten at night. Another contemporary writes : " He devotes himself to accomplishments and amusements day and night, is intent on nothing else, and leaves business to Wolsey, who rules everything."

As a sportsman, Henry was the " *beau idéal* " of his people. In the lists he especially distinguished himself, " in supernatural feats, changing his horses, and making them fly or rather leap, to the delight and ecstasy of everybody."

He also gave himself to masquerades and charades. We are told : " It was at the Christmas festivals at Richmond, that Henry VIII. stole from the side of the Queen during the jousts, and returned in the disguise of a strange Knight, astonishing all the company

with the grace and vigour of his tilting. At
first the King appeared ashamed of taking
part in these gladiatorial exercises, but the
applause he received on all sides soon inclined
him openly to appear on every occasion in
the tilt-yard. Katharine humoured the child-
ish taste of her husband for disguisings and
masquings, by pretending great surprise when
he presented himself before her in some
assumed character."

He was gifted with enormous energy ; he
could ride all day, changing his horses nine
or ten times a day ; then he would dance all
night ; even then his energies were not
exhausted ; then he would write what the
courtiers described as poetry, or he would
compose music, or he would dash off an
attack on Luther, and so earn from the
Pope the much-coveted title of " *Fidei
Defensor.*"

In shooting at the butt, it is said, Henry
excelled, drawing the best bow in England.
At tennis, too, he excelled beyond all others.
He was addicted to games of chance, and his
courtiers permitted him to lose as much as
£3,500 in the course of one year—scarcely a

tactful proceeding. He played with taste and execution on the organ, harpsichord and lute. He had a powerful voice, and sang with great accomplishment.

One of Henry's anthems, " O Lord, the Maker of all thyng," is said to be of the highest merit, and is still sung in our Cathedrals. In his songs,* he particularly liked to dwell on his constancy as a lover :

" As the holly groweth green and never changeth hue,
  So I am—ever have been—unto my lady true."

and again :

" For whoso loveth, should love but one."

An admirable maxim.

As Statesman

In spite of all these distractions, Henry was an excellent man of business in the State—indeed, he threw himself into public affairs with the energy which characterised all his doings. The autocrat only slumbered in Henry; and before many years had

* "Pastime with Good Company," composed and written by Henry, is sung in the production at His Majesty's Theatre.

passed, he threw the enormous energy, which he had hitherto reserved for his pleasure, into affairs of State.

Under Henry, the Navy was first organised as a permanent force. His power of detail was prodigious in this direction. Ever loving the picturesque, even in the most practical affairs of life, Henry " acted as pilot and wore a sailor's coat and trousers, made of cloth of gold, and a gold chain with the inscription, ' *Dieu est mon droit*,' to which was suspended a whistle which he blew nearly as loud as a trumpet." A strange picture !

He was a practical architect, and Whitehall Palace and many other great buildings owed their masonry to his hand.

He spoke French, Spanish, Italian and Latin with great perfection.

He said many wise things. Of the much-debated Divorce, Henry said : " The law of every man's conscience be but a private Court, yet it is the highest and supreme Court for judgment or justice." As the most unjust wars have often produced the greatest heroisms, so the vilest causes have often produced the profoundest utterances.

He appears to have been at peace with himself and complacent towards God. In 1541, during his temporary happiness with Catherine Howard, he attended mass in the chapel, and "receiving his Maker, gave Him most hearty thanks for the good life he led and trusted to lead with his wife; and also desired the Bishop of Lincoln to make like prayer, and give like thanks on All Souls' Day."

Henry confessed his sins every day during the plague. When it abated, his spirits revived, and he wrote daily love-letters to Anne Boleyn, whom he had previously banished from the Court.

As Moralist

A stern moralist in regard to the conduct of others, he had an indulgence towards himself which enabled him somewhat freely to interpret the Divine right of Kings as "*Le droit de seigneur.*" But it is human to tolerate in ourselves the failings which we so rightly deprecate in our inferiors.

So strong was he in his self-assurance, that he made even his conscience his slave.

King Henry VIII

Henry sometimes lacked regal taste. The night Anne Boleyn was executed he supped with Jane Seymour; they were betrothed the next morning, and married ten days later. It is also recorded that on the day following Katharine's death, Henry went to a ball, clad all in yellow.

The commendation or condemnation of Henry's public life depends upon our point of view—upon which side we take in the eternal strife between Church and State.

In this dilemma we must then judge by results, for the truest expression of a man is his work; his greatness or his littleness is measured by his output. Henry produced great results, though he may have been the unconscious instrument of Fate. The motives which guided him in his dealings with the Roman Catholic Church may have been only selfish—they resulted in the emancipation of England from the tyranny of Popedom. A Catholic estimate of him would, of course, have been wholly condemnatory, yet it must be remembered that his quarrel was entirely with the supremacy of the Pope, and that otherwise Henry's Church retained every dogma and every observance believed in and practised by Roman Catholics.

His Greatness

His learning was great, and it was illuminated by his genius. Gradually he learned to control others—to do this he learned to control his temper, when control was useful, but he was always able to make diplomatic use of his rage—a faculty ever helpful in the conduct of one's life! In fact, it is difficult to determine whose genius was greater—Wolsey's as the diplomatist and administrator, or Henry's as the man of action, the figurehead of the State. Around him he gathered the great men of his time, and their learning he turned to his own account, with that adaptiveness which is the peculiar attribute of genius. Shakespeare himself was not more assimilative. In Wolsey, Henry appreciated the mighty minister, and this is one of his claims to greatness, for graciously to permit others to be great is a sign of greatness in a King.

WOLSEY

WOLSEY

His Early Life

Wolsey was born at Ipswich, probably in
the year 1471. His father, Robert Wolsey,
was a grazier, and perhaps also a butcher in
well-to-do circumstances. Sent to Oxford at
the age of 11, at 15 he was made a Bachelor
of Arts. He became a parish priest of St.
Mary's, at Lymington, in 1500. Within a
year he was subjected to the indignity of
being put into the public stocks—for what
reason is not known. It has been said that
he was concerned in a drunken fray. I
prefer to think that, in an unguarded moment,
he had been tempted to speak the truth.
No doubt this was his first lesson in
diplomacy.

In 1507 Wolsey entered the service of
Henry VII. as chaplain, and seems to have
acted as secretary to Richard Fox, Lord
Privy Seal. Thus Wolsey was trained in

the policy of Henry VII., which he never forgot.

His Growing Power

When Henry VIII. came to the throne, he soon realised Wolsey's value, and allowed him full scope for his ambition.

Wolsey thought it desirable to become a Cardinal—a view that was shared by Henry, whose right hand Wolsey had become. In 1514 Henry wrote to the Pope asking that the Hat should be conferred on his favourite, who in the following year was made Lord Chancellor of England. There was some hesitancy which bribery and threats overcame, and in 1515 Wolsey was created Cardinal, in spite of the hatred which Leo X. bore him. Having won this instalment of greatness, Wolsey promptly asked for the Legateship which should give him precedence over the Archbishop of Canterbury. This ambition was realised three years later, but only by what practically amounted to political and ecclesiastical blackmail. In the Church and State Wolsey now stood second only to the King.

HIS STATE

(a) *His Retinue*

As an instance of the state he kept, we are told that he had as many as 500 retainers—among them many lords and ladies. Cavendish, his secretary, describes his pomp when he walked abroad as follows : " First went the Cardinal's attendants, attired in boddices of crimson velvet with gold chains, and the inferior officers in coats of scarlet bordered with black velvet. After these came two gentlemen bearing the great seal and his Cardinal's hat, then two priests with silver pillars and poleaxes, and next two great crosses of silver, whereof one of them was for his Archbishoprick and the other for his legacy borne always before him, whithersoever he went or rode. Then came the Cardinal himself, very sumptuously, on a mule trapped with crimson velvet and his stirrup of copper gilt." Sometimes he preferred to make his progress on the river, for which purpose he had a magnificent State barge " furnished with yeomen standing on the bayles and crowded with his Gentlemen within and without."

His stables were also extensive. His choir far excelled that of the King. Besides all the officials attendant on the Cardinal, Wolsey had 160 personal attendants, including his High Chamberlain, vice-chamberlain; twelve gentlemen ushers, daily waiters; eight gentlemen ushers and waiters of his privy chamber, nine or ten lords, forty persons acting as gentlemen cupbearers, carvers, servers, etc., six yeomen ushers, eight grooms of the chamber, forty-six yeomen of his chamber (one daily to attend upon his person), sixteen doctors and chaplains, two secretaries, three clerks, and four counsellors learned in the law. As Lord Chancellor, he had an additional and separate retinue, almost as numerous, including ministers, armourers, serjeants-at-arms, herald, etc.

(b) Gifts from Foreign Powers

Nor was he above using the gentle suasion of his office to obtain sumptuous gifts from the representatives of foreign powers—for Giustinian, on his return to Venice, reported to the Doge and Senate that "Cardinal Wolsey is very anxious for the signory to send him a hundred Damascene carpets for which he has asked several times, and expected to receive them by the last galleys. This present," continues the diplomat, "might make him pass a decree in our favour; and, at any rate, it would render the Cardinal friendly to our nation in other matters." The carpets, it seems, were duly sent to the Cardinal.

(c) *His Drinking Water*

To show his disregard for money, it may be mentioned that in order to obtain pure water for himself and his household, and not being satisfied with the drinking water at Hampton Court, Wolsey had the water brought from the springs at Coombe Hill by means of leaden pipes, at a cost, it is said, of something like £50,000.

(d) *His Table*

Wolsey seems to have been a lover of good food, for Skelton, for whose verse the Car-

dinal had perhaps expressed contempt,
wrote :

> " To drynke and for to eate
> Swete hypocras* and swete meate
> To keep his flesh chast
> In Lent for a repast
> He eateth capon's stew,
> Fesaunt and partriche mewed
> Hennes checkynges and pygges."

(Skelton, it should be explained, was the Poet
Laureate.) It appears that on this score of
his delicate digestion, Wolsey procured a
dispensation from the Pope for the Lenten
observances.

He had not a robust constitution, and
suffered from many ailments. On one occasion, Henry sent him some pills—it is not
recorded, however, that Wolsey partook of
them.

(e) His Orange

Cavendish speaks of a peculiar habit of
the great Cardinal. He tells us that, " Whenever he was in a crowd or pestered with
suitors, he most commonly held to his nose

* Hypocras—" A favourite medicated drink, compound
of wine, usually red, with spices and sugar."

a very fair orange whereof the meat or sub-
stance within was taken out, and filled up
again with the part of a sponge, wherein was
vinegar and other confections against the
pestilent airs ! " The habit may have given
offence to importunate mayors and others—
the Poet Laureate himself may have been
thus affronted by the imperious Cardinal,
when he wrote :

> " He is set so high
> In his hierarchy
> Of frantic phrenesy
> And foolish fantasy
> That in the Chamber of Stars
> All matters there he mars.
> Clapping his rod on the Board
> No man dare speak a word ;
>   *   *   *   *   *
> Some say " yes " and some
> Sit still as they were dumb.
> Thus thwarting over them,
> He ruleth all the roast
> With bragging and with boast.
> Borne up on every side
> With pomp and with pride."

As a proof of his sensuous tastes, Cavendish
wrote :

" The subtle perfumes of musk and sweet amber
There wanted none to perfume all my chamber."

(f) *His Fool*

That Wolsey, like Henry, was possessed of
a sense of humour we have abundant evidence
in his utterances. Yet he kept a Fool about
him—possibly in order that he might glean
the opinions of the courtiers and common
people. After Wolsey's fall, he sent this Fool
as a present to King Henry. But so loth
was the Fool to leave his master and to suffer
what he considered a social descent, that six
tall yeomen had to conduct him to the
Court; "for," says Cavendish, "the poor
fool took on and fired so in such a rage when
he saw that he must needs depart from my
lord. Yet, notwithstanding, they conveyed
him with Master Norris to the Court, where
the King received him most gladly."*

(g) *Hampton Court*

At his Palace of Hampton Court there were
280 beds always ready for strangers. These
beds were of great splendour, being made
of red, green and russet velvet, satin and
silk, and all with magnificent canopies. The
counterpanes, of which there were many

*It is Wolsey's fool to whom is given the final note
of the play in the production at His Majesty's Theatre.

hundreds, we are told, were of "tawny
damask, lined with blue buckram; blue
damask with flowers of gold; others of red
satin with a great rose in the midst, wrought
with needlework and with garters." Another
is described as "of blue sarcenet, with a tree
in the midst and beastes with scriptures, all
wrought with needlework." The splendour
of these beds beggars all description.

(h) His Plate

His gold and silver plate at Hampton
Court alone, was valued by the Venetian
Ambassador as worth 300,000 golden ducats,
which would be the equivalent in modern
coin of a million and a half! The silver was
estimated at a similar amount. It is said that
the quality was no less striking than the
quantity, for Wolsey insisted on the most
artistic workmanship. He had also a bowl
of gold "with a cover garnished with rubies,
diamonds, pearls and a sapphire set in a
goblet." These gorgeous vessels were deco-
rated with the Cardinal's hat, and sometimes
too, less appropriately perhaps, with images
of Christ!

It is said that the decorations and furniture of Wolsey's Palace were on so splendid a scale that it threw the King's into the shade.

(i) *His Prodigal Splendour*

Like a wise minister, Wolsey did not neglect to entertain the King and keep his mind on trivial things. Hampton Court had become the scene of unrestrained gaiety. Music was always played on these occasions, and the King frequently took part in the revels, dancing, masquerading and singing, accompanying himself on the harpsichord or lute.

The description in Cavendish's " Life of Wolsey " of the famous feast given by the Cardinal to the French ambassadors gives a graphic account of his prodigal splendour. As to the delicacies which were furnished at the supper, Cavendish writes :—

" Anon came up the second course with so many dishes, subtleties and curious devices, which were above a hundred in number, of so goodly proportion and costly, that I suppose the Frenchmen never saw the like. The wonder was no less than it was worthy, indeed. There were castles with images in the same; Paul's Church and steeple, in proportion for the quantity as well counterfeited as the painter should have painted it upon a cloth or wall. There were beasts, birds, fowls of divers kinds, and personages, most lively made and counterfeit in dishes; some fighting, as it were, with swords, some with guns and crossbows; some vaulting and leaping; some dancing with ladies, some in complete harness, justing with spears, and with many more devices than I am able with my wit to describe."

Giustinian, speaking of one of these banquets, writes: "The like of it was never given either by Cleopatra or Caligula." We must remember that Wolsey surrounded himself with such worldly vanities less from any vulgarity in his nature than from a desire to work upon the common mind, ever ready to be impressed by pomp and circumstance.

The Mind of Wolsey

If the outer man was thus caparisoned, what of Wolsey's mind? Its furniture, too, beggared all description. Amiable as Wolsey could be, he could also on occasions be as brusque as his royal master. A contemporary writer says : " I had rather be commanded to Rome than deliver letters to him and wait an answer. When he walks in the Park, he will suffer no suitor to come nigh unto him, but commands him away as far as a man will shoot an arrow."

Yet to others he could be of sweet and gentle disposition and ready to listen and to help with advice.

" Lofty and sour to them that loved him not,
   But to those men that sought him sweet as
      summer."

To those who regard characters as either black or white, Wolsey's was indeed a contradiction. Charges of a personal character have been brought against the great prelate, which need not here be referred to, unless it be to say that if they were true, by so much the less he was a priest, by so much more he was a man

His Ambition

There is no doubt that the Cardinal made several attempts to become Pope—but this enterprise was doomed to failure, although in it he was supported warmly by the King. To gain this end much bribery was needed, " especially to the younger men who are generally the most needy," as the Cardinal said. Wolsey was a sufficiently accomplished social diplomatist to conciliate the young, for their term of office begins to-morrow, and gold is the key of consciences. He was hated and feared, flattered, cajoled and brow-beaten where possible. But as a source of income he was ever held in high regard by the Pope.

His own annual income from bribes—royal and otherwise—was indeed stupendous, though these were received with the knowledge of the King.

So great was the power Wolsey attained to that Fox said of him : " We have to deal with the Cardinal, who is not Cardinal but King." He wrote of himself, " *Ego et rex meus*," and had the initials, " T. W." and the Cardinal's hat stamped on the King's coins. These were among the charges brought against him in his fall.

To his ambitions there was no limit. For the spoils of office he had " an unbounded stomach." As an instance of his pretensions it is recorded that during the festivities of the Emperor's visit to England in 1520, " Wolsey alone sat down to dinner with the royal party, while peers, like the Dukes of Suffolk and Buckingham, performed menial offices for the Cardinal, as well as for Emperor, King and Queen."

When he met Charles at Bruges in 1521 " he treated the Emperor of Spain as an equal. He did not dismount from his mule, but merely doffed his cap, and embraced as a brother the temporal head of Christendom."

" He never granted audience either to English peers or foreign ambassadors " (says Guistinian) " until the third or fourth time of asking." Small wonder that he incurred the hatred of the nobility and the jealousy of the King. During his embassy to France in 1527, it is said that " his attendants served cap in hand, and when bringing the dishes knelt before him in the act of presenting them. Those who waited on the Most Christian King, kept their caps on their heads, dispensing with such exaggerated ceremonies." Had Wolsey's insolence been tempered by his sense of humour, his fall might have been on a softer place, as his Fool is believed to have remarked.

His Policy

In his policy of the reform of the Church, Wolsey dealt as a giant with his gigantic task. To quote a passage from Taunton : " Ignorance, he knew, was the root of most of the mischief of the day; so by education he endeavoured to give men the means to know better. Falsehood can only be expelled by Truth. . . . Had the other prelates of the age realized the true cause of the religious disputes, and how much they themselves were responsible for the present Ignorance, the sacred name of religion would not have had so bloody a record in this country."

Wolsey's idea was, in fact, to bring the clergy in touch with the thought and conditions of the time. It is wonderful to reflect that this one brain should have controlled the secular and ecclesiastical destinies of Christendom.

To reform the Church would seem to have been an almost superhuman undertaking, but to a man of Wolsey's greatness obstacles are

only incentives to energy. He was "eager
to cleanse the Church from the accumulated
evil effects of centuries of human passions."
A great man is stronger than a system, while
he lives; but the system often outlives the
man. Wolsey lived in a time whose very
atmosphere was charged with intrigue. Had
he not yielded to a Government by slaughter,
he would not have existed.

The Cardinal realised that ignorance was
one of the chief causes of the difficulties in
the Church. So with great zeal he devoted
himself to the founding of two colleges, one
in Ipswich, the other in Oxford. His scheme
was never entirely carried out, for on Wolsey's
fall his works were not completed. The
College at Ipswich fell into abeyance, but
his college at Oxford was spared and refounded.
Originally called Cardinal College, it was
renamed Christ Church, so that not even in
name was it allowed to be a memorial of
Wolsey's greatness.

His Genius

For a long time Wolsey was regarded merely
as the type of the ambitious and arrogant

ecclesiastic whom the Reformation had made
an impossibility in the future. It was not
till the mass of documents relating to the
reign of Henry VIII. was published that it
was possible to estimate the greatness of
the Cardinal's schemes. He took a wider
view of the problems of his time than any
statesman had done before. He had a genius
for diplomacy. He was an artist and en-
thusiast in politics. They were not a
pursuit to him, but a passion. Not perhaps unjustly has he been called the greatest
statesman England ever produced.

England, at the beginning of Henry VIII.'s
reign, was weakened after the struggles of the
Civil Wars, and wished to find peace at home
at the cost of obscurity abroad. But it was
this England which Wolsey's policy raised
" from a third-rate state of little account into
the highest circle of European politics."
Wolsey did not show his genius to the best
advantage in local politics, but in diplomacy.
He could only be inspired by the gigantic
things of statecraft. When he was set by
Henry to deal with the sordid matter of the
divorce, he felt restricted and cramped. He

was better as a patriot than as a royal
servant. It was this feeling of being sullied
and unnerved in the uncongenial skirmishings
of the divorce that jarred on his sensitive
nature and made his ambitious hand lose
its cunning. A first-rate man cannot do
second-rate things well.

Henry and Wolsey were two giants littered
in one day. Wolsey had realised his possi-
bilities of power before Henry. But when
Henry once learned how easy it was for
him to get his own way, Wolsey learned
how dependent he necessarily was on the
King's good will. And then, "the nation
which had trembled before Wolsey, learned
to tremble before the King who could destroy
Wolsey with a breath."

Had Wolsey been able to fulfil his own
ideals, had he been the head of a Republic and
not the servant of a King, his public record
would no doubt have been on a higher ethical
plane. That he himself realised this is
shown by his pathetic words to Sir William
Kingston, which have been but slightly
paraphrased by Shakespeare : " Well, well,
Master Kingston, I see how the matter against

me is framed, but if I had served my God as diligently as I have done the King, He would not have given me over in my grey hairs." In this frankness we recognise once again a flicker of greatness—one might almost say a touch of divine humour.

The lives of great men compose themselves dramatically; Wolsey's end was indeed a fit theme for the dramatist.

His Fall

In his later years, Wolsey began to totter on his throne. The King had become more and more masterful. It was impossible for two such stormy men to act permanently in concord. In 1528, Wolsey said that as soon as he had accomplished his ambition of reconciling England and France, and reforming the English laws and settling the succession, "he would retire and serve God for the rest of his days." In 1529 he lost his hold over Parliament and over Henry. The Great Seal was taken from him.

The end of Wolsey was indeed appalling in its sordid tragedy. The woman had prevailed—Anne's revenge was sufficiently complete to satisfy even a woman scorned. The King, too, was probably more inclined to lend a willing ear to her whisperings, since he had grown jealous of his minister's greatness. He paid to his superior the tribute of hatred. Henry, who had treated the Cardinal as his friend and " walked with him in the garden arm in arm and sometimes with his arm thrown caressingly round his shoulder," now felt very differently towards his one-time favourite.

Covetous of Wolsey's splendour, he asked him why he, a subject, should have so magnificent an abode as Hampton Court, whereupon Wolsey diplomatically answered (feeling perhaps the twitch of a phantom rope around his neck), " To show how noble a palace a subject may offer to his sovereign." The King was not slow to accept this offer, and thenceforth made Hampton Court Palace his own.

Wolsey, too, was failing in body—the sharks that follow the ship of State were already scenting their prey. As the King turned his back on Wolsey, Wolsey turned

CARDINAL WOLSEY

From the Portrait by Holbein, at Christ Church, Oxford

his face to God. Accused of high treason
for having acted as Legate, Wolsey pleaded
guilty of the offence, committed with the
approval of the King. He was deprived of
his worldly goods, and retired to his house
at Esher.

Wolsey an Exile from Court

Cavendish says : " My Lord and his family
continued there the space of three or four
weeks without beds, sheets, tablecloths, cups
and dishes to eat our meat, or to lie in."
He was forced to borrow the bare necessaries
of life. The mighty had fallen indeed ! This
was in the year 1529. In his disgrace, he
was without friends. The Pope ignored him.
But Queen Katharine—noble in a kindred
sorrow—sent words of sympathy. Death was
approaching, and Wolsey prepared himself
for the great event by fasting and prayer.
Ordered to York, he arrived at Peterborough
in Easter Week. There it is said : " Upon
Palm Sunday, he went in procession with the
monks, bearing his palm ; setting forth God's
service right honourably with such singing
men as he then had remaining with him.

He Washes the Feet of the Poor

And upon Maundy Thursday he made his Maundy in Our Lady's Chapel, having fifty-nine poor men, whose feet he washed, wiped and kissed; each of these poor men had twelve pence in money, three ells of canvas to make them shirts, a pair of new shoes, a cast of mead, three red herrings, and three white herrings, and the odd person had two shillings. Upon Easter Day he rode to the Resurrection,* and that morning he went in procession in his Cardinal's vesture, with his hat and hood on his head, and he himself sang there the High Mass very devoutly, and granted Clean Remission to all the hearers, and there continued all the holidays."

Arrived at York, he indulged with a difference in his old love of hospitality; "he kept a noble house and plenty of both meat and drink for all comers, both for rich and poor, and much alms given at his gates. He used much charity and pity among his poor tenants and others." This

---

* The ceremony of bringing the Blessed Sacrament from the sepulchre where it had lain since the Good Friday. This took place early on Easter Monday.

caused him to be beloved in the country, Those that hated him owing to his repute learned to love him—he went among the people and brought them food and comforted them in their troubles. Now he was loved among the poor as he had been feared among the great.

Condemned to the Tower

On the 4th November, he was arrested on a new charge of high treason and condemned to the Tower. He left under custody amid the lamentations of the poor people, who in their thousands crowded round him, crying "God save your Grace! God save your Grace! The foul evil take all them that hath thus taken you from us! We pray God that a very vengeance may light upon them." He remained at Sheffield Park, the Earl of Shrewsbury's seat, for eighteen days. Here his health broke down. There arrived, with twenty-four of the Guard from London, Sir William Kingston with order to conduct him to the Tower. The next day, in spite of increasing illness, he set out, but he could hardly ride his mule.

His End

Reaching the Abbey at Leicester on the 26th of November, and being received by the Benedictine monks, he said : " Father Abbot, I am come hither to leave my bones among you." Here he took to his last bed, and made ready to meet his God.

The following morning, the 29th of November, he who had trod the ways of glory and sounded all the depths and shoals of honour, he who had shaped the destinies of Empires, before whom Popes and Parliaments had trembled, he who had swathed himself in the purple of kingdom, of power and of glory, learned the littleness of greatness and entered the Republic of Death in a hair-shirt.

KATHARINE

KATHARINE

For purity and steadfastness of devotion and duty, Katharine stands unsurpassed in the history of the world, and Shakespeare has conceived no more pathetic figure than that of the patient Queen living in the midst of an unscrupulous Court.

Daughter of Ferdinand and Isabella of Spain, she was betrothed at the age of five to Arthur, Henry VII.'s eldest son. Though known as the Princess of Wales, it was not till 1501, when only sixteen years old, that she was married to Prince Arthur. She had scarcely been married six months when Arthur died, at the early age of fifteen, and she was left a widow. Henry VII., in his desire to keep her marriage dower of 200,000 crowns, proposed a marriage between her and Arthur's brother. Katharine wrote to her father saying she had " no inclination for a second marriage in England." In spite of her remonstrances and the misgivings

of the Pope, who had no wish to give
the necessary dispensation for her to marry
her deceased husband's brother, she was
betrothed to Henry after two years of
widowhood. But it was not till a few months
after Henry VIII. came to the throne, five
years later, that they were actually married.
Henry was five years younger than Katharine,
but their early married life appears to have
been very happy. She wrote to her father,
" Our time is ever passed in continual
feasts."

The cruel field sports of the time the Queen
never could take any delight in, and avoided
them as much as possible. She was pious
and ascetic and most proficient in needlework.
Katharine had a number of children, all of
whom died shortly after birth. It was this
consideration in the first instance which
weighed in Henry's mind in desiring a divorce.
The first child to survive was Princess Mary,
born in February, 1516. Henry expressed the
hope that sons would follow. But Katharine
had no further living children. Henry hoped
against hope, and undertook, in the event of
her having an heir, to lead a crusade against

the Turks. Even this bribe to fortune
proved unavailing. Henry's conscience, which
was at best of the utilitarian sort, now
began to suffer deep pangs, and in 1525,
when Katharine was forty years old and he
thirty-four, he gave up hope of the much-
needed heir to the throne. The Queen herself
thought her childlessness was " a judgment
of God, for that her former marriage was
made in blood," the innocent Earl of Warwick
having been put to death owing to the
demand of Ferdinand of Aragon.

The King began to indulge in the super-
stition that his marriage with a brother's
widow was marked with the curse of Heaven.
It is perhaps a strange coincidence that
Anne Boleyn should have appeared on the
scene at this moment. Katharine seems
always to have regarded her rival with
charity and pity. When one of her gentlewomen began to curse Anne as the cause of
the Queen's misery, the Queen stopped her.
" Curse her not," she said, " but rather pray
for her ; for even now is the time fast coming
when you shall have reason to pity her and
lament her case."

Undoubtedly Katharine's most notable quality was her dignity. Even her enemies regarded her with respect. She was always sustained by the greatness of her soul, her life of right doing and her feeling of being " a Queen and daughter of a King." Through all her bitter trials she went, a pathetic figure, untouched by calumny. If she had any faults they are certainly not recorded in history. Her farewell letter to the King would seem to be very characteristic of Katharine's beauty of character. She knew the hand of death was upon her. She had entreated the King, but Henry had refused her request for a last interview with her daughter Mary.

With this final cruelty fresh in her mind she still could write : " My lord and dear husband,—I commend me unto you. The hour of my death draweth fast on, and my case being such, the tender love I owe you forceth me with a few words, to put you in remembrance of the health and safeguard of your soul, which you ought to prefer before all worldly matters, and before the care and tendering of your own body,

for the which you have cast me into many
miseries and yourself into many cares. For
my part I do pardon you all, yea, I do wish
and devoutly pray God that He will pardon
you."

ANNE BOLEYN

ANNE BOLEYN

The estimation of the character of Anne Boleyn would seem to be as varied as the spelling of her name. She is believed to have been born in 1507. The Boleyns or Bullens were a Norfolk family of French origin, but her mother was of noble blood, being daughter of the Earl of Ormonde, and so a descendant of Edward I. It is a curious fact that all of Henry's wives can trace their descent from this King. Of Anne's early life little is known save that she was sent as Maid of Honour to the French Queen Claude. She was probably about nineteen years old when she was recalled to the English Court and began her round of revels and love intrigues. Certainly she was a born leader of men ; many have denied her actual beauty, but she had the greater quality of charm, the power of subjugating, the beckoning eye. An accomplished dancer, we read of her " as leaping and jumping with infinite grace and agility.". " She dressed with marvellous taste and devised new robes," but of the ladies who copied her, we read that unfortunately " none wore them with her gracefulness, in which she rivalled Venus." Music, too, was added to her accomplishments, and Cavendish tells us how " when she composed her hands to play and her voice to sing, it was joined with that sweetness of countenance that three harmonies concurred."

It is difficult to speak with unalloyed admiration of Anne's virtue. At the most charitable computation, she was an outrageous flirt. It would seem that she was genuinely in love with Lord Percy, and that Wolsey was ordered by the then captivated and jealous King to put an end to their intrigue and their desire to marry. Anne is supposed never to have forgiven Wolsey for this, and by a dramatic irony it was her former lover, Percy, then become Earl of Northumberland, who was sent to arrest the fallen Cardinal at York. It is said that he treated Wolsey in a brutal manner, having his legs bound to the stirrup of his mule like a common criminal. When

Henry, in his infatuation for the attractive Lady-in-Waiting to his Queen, as she was then, wished Wolsey to become the aider and abettor of his love affairs, Wolsey found himself placed in the double capacity of man of God and man of Kings. In these cases, God is apt to go to the wall—for the time being. But it was Wolsey's vain attempt to serve two masters that caused his fall, which the French Ambassador attributed entirely to the ill offices of Anne Boleyn. This is another proof that courtiers should always keep on the right side of women.

Nothing could stop Henry's passion for Anne, and she showed her wonderful cleverness in the way she kept his love alive for years, being first created Marchioness of Pembroke, and ultimately triumphing over every obstacle and gaining her wish of being his Queen. This phase of her character has been nicely touched by Shakespeare's own deft hand. She was crowned with unparalleled splendour on Whit Sunday of 1533. At the banquet held after the Coronation of Anne Boleyn, we read that two Countesses stood on either side of Anne's chair and often held a "fine cloth before the Queen's face whenever she listed to spit." "And under the table went two gentlewomen, and sat at the Queen's feet during the dinner." The courtier's life, like the burglar's does not appear to have been one of unmixed happiness.

In the same year she bore Henry a child, but to everyone's disappointment, it proved to be a girl, who was christened Elizabeth, and became the great Queen of England. Anne's triumph was pathetically brief. Her most important act was that of getting the publication of the Bible author-ised in England. Two years after her coro-nation, Sir Thomas More, who had refused to swear fealty to the King's heir by Anne, who had been thrown into prison and was awaiting execution, asked "How Queen Anne did?" "There is nothing else but dancing and sporting," was the answer. "These dances of hers," he said, "will prove such dances that she will spurn our heads off like footballs, but it will not be long ere her head dance the like dance." In a year's time, this prophecy came true. Her Lady-in-Waiting, the beautiful Jane Seymour, stole the King from her who in her time had betrayed her royal mistress.

There are two versions with regard to her last feelings towards the King. Lord Bacon writes that just before her execution she said : " Commend me to his Majesty and tell him he hath ever been constant in his career of advancing me. From a private gentlewoman he made me a marchioness, from a marchioness a Queen ; and now he hath left no higher degree of honour, he gives my innocency the crown of martyrdom." This contains a fine sting of satire. Another chronicler gives us her words as follows : " I pray God to save the King, and send him long to reign over you, for a gentler or more merciful prince was there never." One cannot but think that this latter version of her dying words may have been edited by his Grace of Canterbury.

If it is difficult to reconcile Anne's heartlessness with her piety, it should be remembered that cruelty is often the twin-sister of religious fervour.

Whatever may have been her failings of

character, whatever misfortunes she may have suffered during her life, Anne will ever live in history as one of the master mistresses of the world.

THE DIVORCE

THE DIVORCE

As to the divorce, it will be well to clear away the enormous amount of argument, of vituperation and prevarication by which the whole question is obscured, and to seek by the magnet of common sense to find the needle of truth in this vast bundle of hay.

The situation was complicated. In those days it was generally supposed that no woman could succeed to the throne, and a male successor was regarded as a political necessity. Charles V., too, was plotting to depose Henry and to proclaim James V. as ruler of England, or Mary, who was to be married to an English noble for this purpose.

The Succession

The Duke of Buckingham was the most formidable possible heir to the throne, were the King to die without male heirs. His execution took place in 1521. Desperate men take desperate remedies. Now, in 1519, Henry had a natural son by Elizabeth Blount, sister of Lord Mountjoy. This boy Henry contemplated placing on the throne, so causing considerable uneasiness to the Queen. In 1525 he was created Duke of Richmond. Shortly after he was made Lord High Admiral of England and Lord Lieutenant of Ireland. It was suggested that he should marry a royal Princess. Another suggestion was that he should marry his half-sister, an arrangement which seems to have commended itself to the Pope, on condition that Henry abandoned his divorce from Queen Katharine! But this was not to be, and Mary was betrothed to the French prince. An heir must be obtained somehow, and the divorce, therefore, took more and more tangible shape. A marriage with Anne Boleyn was the next move. To attain this object, Henry applied himself with his accustomed energy. His conscience walked hand in hand with expediency.

To Rome, Henry sent many embassies and to the Universities of Christendom much gold, in order to persuade them to yield to the dictates of his conscience. His passion for marriage lines in his amours was one of Henry's most distinguishing qualities.

In 1527 an union between Francis I. and the Princess Mary was set on foot. Here the question of Mary's legitimacy was debated, and this gave Henry another excuse for regarding the divorce as necessary.

As the modern historian might aptly say: "Here was a pretty kettle of fish."

There can be little doubt that as a man of God, Wolsey strongly disapproved of the divorce, but as the King's Chancellor he felt himself bound to urge his case to the best of his ability. He was in fact the advocate— the devil's advocate—under protest. One cannot imagine a more terrible position for a man of conscience to be placed in, but once even a cardinal embarks in politics the working of his conscience is temporarily suspended. In world politics the Ten Commandments are apt to become a negligible quantity.

Henry's conscience was becoming more and more tender. Much may be urged in favour of the divorce from a political point of view, and no doubt Henry had a powerful faculty of self-persuasion—such men can grow to believe that whatever they desire is right, that "there is nothing either good or bad but thinking makes it so." It is a pity, however, that Henry's scruples did not assert themselves before the marriage with Katharine took place, for the ethical arguments against such an union were then equally strong. Indeed, these scruples appear to have been a "family failing," for Henry's sister Margaret, Queen of Scotland, obtained a dispensation of divorce from Rome on far slenderer grounds. To make matters worse for Henry, Rome was sacked—the Pope was a prisoner in the Emperor's hands. In this state of things, the Pope was naturally disinclined to give offence to the Emperor by divorcing his aunt (Katharine).

At all costs, the Pope must be set free— on this errand Wolsey now set out for France. But Charles V. was no less wily than Wolsey, and dispatched Cardinal Quignon to Rome to frustrate his endeavours, and to deprive Wolsey of his legatine powers. A schism between Henry and Wolsey was now asserting itself—Wolsey being opposed to the King's union with Anne Boleyn. ("We'll no Anne Boleyns for him!") Wolsey desired that the King should marry the French King's sister, in order to strengthen his opposition to Charles V. of Spain.

The Cardinal was indeed in an unenviable position. If the divorce succeeded, then his enemy, Anne Boleyn, would triumph and he would fall. If the divorce failed, then Henry would thrust from him the agent who had failed to secure the object of his master. And in his fall the Cardinal would drag down the Church. It is said that Wolsey secretly opposed the divorce. This is fully brought out in Shakespeare's play, and is indeed the main cause of Wolsey's fall.

There was for Henry now only one way out of the dilemma into which the power of the Pope had thrown him—that was to obtain a dispensation for a bigamous marriage. It seems that Henry himself cancelled the proposition before it was made. This scruple was unnecessary, for the Pope himself secretly made a proposition " that His Majesty might be allowed two wives."

The sanction for the marriage with Anne Boleyn was obtained without great difficulty —but it was to be subject to the divorce from Katharine being ratified. Thus the King was faced with another obstacle. At this moment began the struggle for supremacy at Rome between English and Spanish influence. The Pope had to choose between the two ; Charles V. was the victor, whereupon Henry cut the Gordian knot by throwing over the jurisdiction of Rome. Wolsey was in a position of tragic perplexity. He was torn by his allegiance to the King, and his zeal for the preservation of the Church. He wrote : " I cannot reflect upon it and close my eye, for I see ruin, infamy and subversion of the whole dignity and estimation of the See Apostolic if this course is persisted in." But Pope Clement dared not offend the Emperor Charles, who was his best, because his most powerful ally, and had he not proved his power by sacking Rome ? The Pope, although quite ready to grant dispensations for a marriage of Princess Mary and her half-brother, the Duke of Richmond, though he was ready to grant Margaret's divorce,

could not afford to stultify the whole Papal
dignity by revoking the dispensation he had
originally given that Henry should marry his
brother's wife. Truly an edifying embroglio!
Henry was desirous of shifting the responsibility on God through the Pope—the Pope
was sufficiently astute to wish to put the
responsibility on the devil through Henry.
There was one other course open—that
course the Pope took.

In 1528 he gave a Commission to Wolsey
and Cardinal Campeggio to try the case
themselves, and pronounce sentence. Back
went the embassy to England. Wolsey saw
through the device, for the Pope was still free
to revoke the Commission. Indeed Clement's
attitude towards Henry was dictated entirely
by the fluctuating fortune of Charles V.,
Emperor of Spain. Meanwhile, Charles won
another battle against the French, and the
Pope at once gave secret instructions to
Campeggio to procrastinate, assuring Charles
that nothing would be done which should be
to the detriment of Katharine. The wily Campeggio (emissary of the Pope) at first sought
to persuade Henry to refrain from the divorce.

Henry refused. Thereupon he endeavoured
to persuade Katharine voluntarily to enter
a nunnery. Among all these plotters and
intriguers, Katharine, adamant in her virtue,
maintained her position as lawful wife and
Queen.

When Wolsey and Campeggio visited the
Queen she was doing needlework with her
maids. It appears (and this is important as
showing the inwardness of Wolsey's attitude
in the matter of the divorce) that " from this
interview the Queen gained over both legates
to her cause ; indeed, they would never
pronounce against her, and this was the head
and front of the King's enmity to his former
favourite Wolsey." In the first instance,
Wolsey was undoubtedly a party, however
unwilling, to the separation of the King and
Queen, in order that Henry might marry
the brilliant and high-minded sister of
Francis I., Duchess of Alençon. That lady
would not listen to such a proposal, lest it
should break the heart of Queen Katharine.
Wolsey was, either from personal enmity towards Anne Boleyn or from his
estimate of her character, or from both,

throughout opposed to the union with that lady.

Subsequently the King sent to Katharine a deputation from his Council announcing that he had, by the advice of Cranmer, obtained the opinions of the universities of Europe concerning the divorce, and found several which considered it expedient. He therefore entreated her, for the quieting of his conscience, that she would refer the matter to the arbitration of four English prelates and four nobles. The Queen received the message in her chamber, and replied to it: "God grant my husband a quiet conscience, but I mean to abide by no decision excepting that of Rome." This infuriated the King.

After many delays and the appearance of a document which was declared by one side to be a forgery, and by the other to be genuine, the case began on May 31, 1529. In the great hall of Blackfriars both the King and Queen appeared in person to hear the decision of the Court. The trial itself is very faithfully rendered in Shakespeare's play. Finding the King obdurate, Katharine protested against the jurisdiction of the

Court, and appealing finally to Rome, with-drew from Blackfriars.

Judgment was to be delivered on the 23rd of July, 1529. Campeggio rose in the presence of the King and adjourned the Court till October. This was the last straw, and the last meeting of the Court. Henry had lost. Charles was once more in the ascendant. England and France had declared war on him in 1528, but England's heart was not in the enterprise—the feeling of hatred to Wolsey became widespread. Henry and Charles made terms of peace, and embraced once more after a bloodless and (for England) somewhat ignominious war. The French force was utterly defeated in battle. The Pope and Charles signed a treaty—all was nicely arranged. The Pope's nephew was to marry the Emperor's natural daughter; certain towns were to be restored to the Pope, who was to crown Charles with the Imperial crown. The participators in the sacking of Rome were to be absolved from sin; the proceedings against the Emperor's aunt, Katharine, were to be null and void. If Katharine could not obtain justice in England,

The Divorce

Henry should not have his justice in Rome.
The Pope and the Emperor kissed again, and
Henry finally cut himself adrift from Rome.
It was the failure of the divorce that made
England a Protestant country.

Henry now openly defied the Pope, by whom
he was excommunicated, and so " deprived
of the solace of the rites of religion ; when he
died he must lie without burial, and in hell
suffer torment for ever." The mind shrinks
from contemplating the tortures to which
the soul of His Majesty might have been
subjected but for the timely intervention of
his Grace the Archbishop of Canterbury.

So far from Henry suffering in a temporal
sense, he continued to defy the opinion and
the power of the world. He showed his greatness by looking public opinion unflinchingly
in the face; by ignoring, he conquered it.
Amid the thunderous roarings of the Papal
bull, Henry stood—as we see him in his
picture—smiling and indifferent. " I never
saw the King merrier than now," wrote a contemporary in 1533. Henry always had good
cards—now he held the ace of public
opinion up his sleeve.

Wolsey, although averse to the Queen's divorce and the marriage of Anne Boleyn, expressed himself in terms of the strongest opposition to the overbearing Pope. A few days before the Papal revocation arrived, the Cardinal wrote thus : " If the King be cited to appear at Rome in person or by proxy, and his prerogative be interfered with, none of his subjects will tolerate it. If he appears in Italy, it will be at the head of a formidable army." Opposed as they were to the divorce, the English people were of one mind with Wolsey in this attitude.

Henry was not slow to avail himself of the new development, and he made the divorce become in the eyes of the people but a secondary consideration to the pride of England. He drew the red herring of the Reformation across the trail of the divorce. The King and his Parliament held that the Church should not meddle with temporal affairs. The Church was the curer of souls, not the curer of the body politic.

Katharine's cause sank into the background. The voice of justice was drowned by the birth shrieks of the Reformation.

KATHARINE OF ARAGON
From the Portrait in the National Portrait Gallery

THE REFORMATION

THE REFORMATION

We must remind ourselves that the divorce was merely the irritation which brought the discontent with Rome to a head. Religious affairs were in a very turbulent state. The monasteries were corrupt. The rule of Rome had become political, not spiritual. Luther had worked at shattering the pretensions of the Pope in Europe. Wolsey had prepared the English to acquiesce in Henry's religious supremacy by his long tenure of the whole Papal authority within the realm and the consequent suspension of appeals to Rome. Translations of the New Testament were being secretly read throughout the country—a most dangerous innovation—and Anne Boleyn, who had no cause to love the Pope or his power, held complete sway over the King.

She and her father were said to be " more Lutheran than Luther himself." Though Henry was anti-Papal, he was never anti-Catholic, but, as the representative of God, as head of his own Church, he claimed to take precedence of the Pope. Moreover, the spoliation of the Church was not an unprofitable business.

Rome declared the divorce illegal. Henry, with the support of his Parliament, abolished all forms of tribute to Rome, arranged that the election of Bishops should take place without the interference of the Pope, and declared that if he did not consent to the King's wishes within three months, the whole of his authority in England should be transferred to the Crown. This conditional abolition of the Papal authority was in due course made absolute, and the King assumed the title of Head of the Church.

" The breach with Rome " was effected with a cold and calculated cunning, which the most adept disciple of Machiavelli could not have excelled."—(Pollard.)

With an adroitness amounting to genius, Henry now used the moral suasion (not to use an uglier word) of threats towards the Church to induce the Pope to relent and to assent to the divorce. One by one, in this deadly battle, did the Pope's prerogatives vanish, until the sacerdotal foundations of Rome, so far as England was concerned, had been levelled to the ground.

After many further political troubles and intrigues Henry prevailed on Cranmer, now Archbishop of Canterbury, as head of the Church, to declare the marriage between himself and Katharine to be null and void, and five days later Cranmer declared that Henry and Anne Boleyn were lawfully married. On the 1st of June, 1533, the Archbishop crowned Anne as Queen in Westminster Abbey. Shortly after she gave birth to a daughter, who was christened Elizabeth, and became Queen of England.

Beyond this incident, with which the strange eventful history of Shakespeare's play ends, it is not proposed to travel in these notes, which are but intended as a brief chronicle that may guide the play-goer of to-day (sometimes a hasty reader) to realize the conditions of Henry's reign.

MANNERS AND CUSTOMS

MANNERS AND CUSTOMS

In the days of Henry VIII., the ways of
society differed from our own more in observance than in spirit. Though the gay world
danced and gambled very late, they rose very
early. Their conversation was coarse and
lacked reserve. The ladies cursed freely.
Outward show and ceremony were considered
of the utmost importance. Hats were worn
by the men in church and at meals, and only
removed in the presence of the King and
Cardinal. Kissing was far more prevalent as
a mode of salutation. The Court society
spent the greater part of their income on
clothes. To those in the King's set, a
thousand pounds was nothing out of the
way to spend on a suit of clothes. The
predominant colours at Court were crimson
and green; the Tudor colours were green
and white. It was an age of magnificent
plate, and the possession and display of
masses of gold and silver plate was considered

as a sign of power. Later on in Shakespeare's time, not only the nobles, but also the better class citizens boasted collections of plate.

A quaint instance of the recognition of distinctions of rank is afforded by certain " Ordinances " that went forth as the " Bouche of Court." Thus a Duke or Duchess was allowed in the morning one chet loaf, one manchet and a gallon of ale ; in the afternoon one manchet and one gallon of ale ; and for after supper one chet loaf, one manchet, one gallon of ale and a pitcher of wine, besides torches, etc. A Countess, however, was allowed nothing at all after supper, and a gentleman usher had no allowance for morning or afternoon. These class distinctions must have weighed heavily upon humbler beings, such as Countesses ; but perhaps they consumed more at table to make up for these after-meal deficiencies.

Table manners were a luxury as yet undreamed of. The use of the fork was a new fashion just being introduced from France and Spain.

A NOTE ON THE PRODUCTION OF HENRY VIII. AT HIS MAJESTY'S THEATRE

A NOTE ON THE PRODUCTION OF HENRY VIII. AT HIS MAJESTY'S THEATRE

From the descriptions which have appeared in these pages, it will be seen that the period of Henry VIII. was characterized by great sumptuousness ; indeed, the daily life of the Court consisted largely of revels, masques and displays of splendour.

Henry VIII. is largely a pageant play. As such it was conceived and written, as such we shall endeavour to present it to the public. Indeed, it is obvious that it would be far better not to produce the play at all than to do so without those adjuncts, by which alone the action of the play can be illustrated. Of course, it is not possible to do more than indicate on the stage the sumptuousness of the period of history covered by the play ; but it is hoped that an impression will be conveyed to our own time of Henry in his habit as he lived, of his people, of the architecture, and of the manners and customs of that great age.

The Text

It has been thought desirable to omit almost in their entirety those portions of the play which deal with the Reformation, being as they are practically devoid of dramatic interest and calculated, as they are, to weary an audience. In taking this course, I feel the less hesitation as there can be no doubt that all these passages were from the first omitted in Shakespeare's own representations of the play.

We have incontrovertible evidence that in Shakespeare's time, Henry VIII. was played in " two short hours."

> ". . . Those that come to see
> Only a show or two and so agree
> The play may pass. If they be still and willing
> I'll undertake may see away their shilling
> Richly in two short hours."

These words, addressed to the audience in the prologue, make it quite clear that a considerable portion of the play was considered by the author to be superfluous to the dramatic action—and so it is. Acted without any waits whatsoever, Henry VIII., as it is written, would take at least three hours and a half in the playing. Although we are not able to compass the performance within the prescribed "two short hours," for we show a greater respect for the preservation of the text than did Shakespeare himself, an attempt will be made to confine the absolute spoken words as nearly as possible within the time prescribed in the prologue.

In the dramatic presentation of the play, there are many passages of intensely moving interest, the action and characters are drawn with a remarkable fidelity to the actualities. As has been suggested, however, the play depends more largely than do most of Shakespeare's works on those outward displays which an attempt will be made to realize on the stage.

Shakespeare as Stage Manager

That Shakespeare, as a stage-manager, availed himself as far as possible of these adjuncts is only too evident from the fact that it was the firing off the cannon which caused a conflagration and the consequent burning down of the Globe Theatre. The destruction of the manuscripts of Shakespeare's plays was probably due to this calamity. The incident shows a lamentable love of stage-mounting for which some of the critics of the time no doubt took the poet severely to task. In connection with the love of pageantry which then prevailed, it is well known that Shakespeare and Ben Jonson were wont to arrange the Masques which were so much in vogue in their time.

The Fire

The Globe Theatre was burnt on June 29th, 1613. Thomas Lorkins, in a letter to Sir Thomas Puckering on June 30th, says : " No longer since than yesterday, while Bourbidge his companie were acting at ye Globe the play of Henry 8, and there shooting of certayne chambers in way of triumph ; the fire catch and fastened upon the thatch of ye house and there burned so furiously as it consumed ye whole house all in lesse than two hours, the people having enough to doe to save themselves."

Other Productions of the Play

There are records of many other productions of Henry VIII. existing. In 1663 it was produced at Lincoln's Inn Fields as a pageant play. The redoubtable Mr. Pepys visited this production, without appearing to have enjoyed the play. In contrast to him, old Dr. Johnson said that whenever Mrs. Siddons played the part of Katharine, he would "hobble to the theatre to see her."

In 1707, Henry VIII. was produced at the Haymarket, with an exceptionally strong cast; in 1722 it was done at Drury Lane, in which production Booth played Henry VIII.

In 1727 it was again played at Drury Lane. On this occasion the spectacle of the Coronation of Anne Boleyn was added, on which one scene, we are told, £1,000 had been expended. It will come to many as a surprise that so much splendour and so large an expenditure of money were at that time lavished on the stage. The play had an exceptional run of forty nights, largely owing, it is said, to the popularity it obtained through the Coronation of George II., which had taken place a few weeks before.

The play was a great favourite of George II. and was in consequence frequently revived during his reign. On being asked by a grave nobleman, after a performance at Hampton Court, how the King liked it, Sir Richard Steele replied: " So terribly well, my lord, that I was afraid I should have lost all my actors, for I was not sure the King would not keep them to fill the posts at Court that he saw them so fit for in the play."

In 1744, Henry VIII. was given for the first time at Covent Garden, but was not revived until 1772, when it was announced at Covent Garden as " 'Henry VIII.,' not acted for 20 years." The Coronation was again introduced."

Queen Katharine was one of Mrs. Siddons' great parts. She made her first appearance in this character at Drury Lane in 1788. In 1808 it was again revived, and Mrs. Siddons once more played the Queen, Kemble appearing as Wolsey.

In 1822, Edmund Kean made his first appearance as Wolsey at Drury Lane, but the play was only given four times.

In 1832, the play was revived at Covent Garden with extraordinary splendour, and a magnificent cast. Charles Kemble played King Henry ; Mr. Young, Wolsey ; Miss Ellen Tree, Anne Boleyn ; and Miss Fanny Kemble appeared for the first time as Queen Katharine. Her success seems to have been great. We are told that Miss Ellen Tree, as Anne Boleyn, appeared to great disadvantage ; " her headdress was the most frightful and unbecoming thing imaginable, though we believe it was taken from one of Holbein's." In those days correctness of costume was considered most lamentable and most laughable. In this production, too, the Coronation was substituted for the procession. The criticism adds that " during the progress of the play the public seized every opportunity of showing their dislike of the Bishops, and the moment they came on the stage they were assailed with hissing and hooting, and one of the prelates. in his haste to escape from such a reception, fell prostrate, which excited bursts of merriment from all parts of the house."

In 1855, Charles Kean revived the play with his accustomed care and sumptuousness. In this famous revival Mrs. Kean appeared as " Queen Katharine."

Irving's Production

Sir Henry Irving's magnificent production will still be fresh in the memory of many playgoers. It was admitted on all hands to be an artistic achievement of the highest kind, and Sir Henry Irving was richly rewarded by the support of the public, the play running 203 nights. Miss Ellen Terry greatly distinguished herself in the part of Queen Katharine, contributing in no small degree to the success of the production. Sir Henry Irving, in the part of Wolsey, made a deep impression. Mr. William Terriss played the King. Mr. Forbes Robertson made a memorable success in the part of Buckingham ; and it is interesting to note that Miss Violet Vanbrugh played the part of Anne Boleyn.

ANNE BOLEYN
From the Portrait by Holbein, at Warwick Castle

A Note on Production

The Music

An outstanding feature of the Lyceum production was Edward German's music. I deem myself fortunate that this music was available for the present production. It may be mentioned that Mr. German has composed some additional numbers, amongst which is the Anthem sung in the Coronation of Anne Boleyn.

Shakespeare's Accuracy of Detail

I cannot help quoting one passage from Cavendish at length to show how closely Shakespeare keeps to the chronicles of his time. It will be found that Scene 8 of Act I. is practically identical with the following description :—

The banquets were set forth, with masks and mummeries, in so gorgeous a sort, and costly manner, that it was a heaven to behold.
. . . I have seen the king suddenly come in thither in a mask, with a dozen of other maskers, all in garments like shepherds.
. . . And at his coming and before he came into the hall, ye shall understand that he came

by water to the water gate, without any noise; where, against his coming, were laid charged many chambers, and at his landing they were all shot off, which made such a rumble in the air, that it was like thunder. It made all the noblemen, ladies and gentlewomen to muse what it should mean coming so suddenly, they sitting quietly at a solemn banquet. Then immediately after this great shot of guns, the cardinal desired the Lord Chamberlain, and Comptroller, to look what this sudden shot should mean, as though he knew nothing of the matter. They thereupon looking out of the windows into Thames, returned again, and showed him, that it seemed to them there should be some noblemen and strangers arrived at his bridge, as ambassadors from some foreign prince. With that, quoth the Cardinal, " I shall desire you, because ye can speak French, to take the pains to go down into the hall to encounter and to receive them, according to their estates, and to conduct them into this chamber, where they shall see us, and all these noble personages sitting merrily at our banquet, desiring them to sit down with us and to take part of our fare and pastime." Then they went incontinent down into the hall, where they received them with twenty new torches, and conveyed them up into the chamber, with such a number of drums and fifes as I have seldom seen together, at one time in any masque. At their arrival into the chamber, two and two together, they went directly before the cardinal where he sat, saluting him very reverently, to whom the Lord Chamberlain for them said : " Sir,

A Note on Production

forasmuch as they be strangers, and can speak no English, they have desired me to declare unto your Grace thus : they, having understanding of this your triumphant banquet, where was assembled such a number of excellent fair dames, could do no less, under the supportation of your good grace, but to repair hither to view as well their incomparable beauty, as for to accompany them to mumchance, and then after to dance with them, and so to have of them acquaintance. And, sir, they furthermore require of your Grace licence to accomplish the cause of their repair." To whom the Cardinal answered, that he was very well contented they should do so. Then the masquers went first and saluted all the dames as they sat, and then returned to the most worthiest.

. . . Then quoth the Cardinal to my Lord Chamberlain, " I pray you," quoth he, " show them that it seemeth me that there should be among them some noble man, whom I suppose to be much more worthy of honour to sit and occupy this room and place than I ; to whom I would most gladly, if I knew him, surrender my place according to my duty." Then spake my Lord Chamberlain, unto them in French, declaring my Lord Cardinal's mind, and they rounding him again in the ear, my Lord Chamberlain said to my Lord Cardinal, " Sir, they confess," quoth he, " that among them there is such a noble personage, whom, if your Grace can appoint him from the other, he is contented to disclose himself, and to accept your place most worthily." With that the cardinal, taking a good advisement among them, at the last, quoth he, " Me seemeth the gentleman with the black beard should be even he." And with that he arose out of his chair, and offered the same to the gentleman in the black beard, with his cap in his hand. The person to whom he offered then his chair was Sir Edward Neville, a comely knight of goodly personage, that much more resembled the king's person in that mask, than any other. The king, hearing and perceiving the cardinal so deceived in his estimation and choice, could not forbear laughing ; but plucked down his visor, and Master Neville's also, and dashed out with such a pleasant countenance and cheer, that all noble estates there assembled, seeing the king to be there amongst them, rejoiced very much.

If Shakespeare could be so true to the actualities, why should not we seek to realise the scene so vividly described by the chronicler and the dramatist ?

In my notes and conclusions on " Henry VIII. and his Court," I have been largely indebted to the guidance of the following books :—

Ernest Law's " History of Hampton Court " ; Strickland's " Queens of England " ; Taunton's " Thomas Wolsey, Legate and Reformer " ; and Cavendish's " Life of Wolsey."

AN APOLOGY AND A FOOTNOTE

AN APOLOGY AND A FOOTNOTE

Here I am tempted to hark back to the modern manner of producing Shakespeare, and to say a few words in extenuation of those methods, which have been assailed in a recent article with almost equal brilliancy and vehemence.

The writer tells us that there are two different kinds of plays, the realistic and the symbolic. Shakespeare's plays, we are assured, belong to the latter category. " The scenery," it is insisted, " not only may, but should be imperfect." This seems an extraordinary doctrine, for if it be right that a play should be imperfectly mounted, it follows that it should be imperfectly acted, and further that it should be imperfectly written. The modern methods, we are assured, employed in the production of Shakespeare, do not properly illustrate the play, but are merely made for vulgar display, with the result of crushing the

author and obscuring his meaning. In this
assertion, I venture to think that our critic
is mistaken; I claim that not the least important mission of the modern theatre is to
give to the public representations of history
which shall be at once an education and a
delight. To do this, the manager should avail
himself of the best archæological and artistic
help his generation can afford him, while
endeavouring to preserve what he believes to
be the spirit and the intention of the author.

It is of course possible for the technically
informed reader to imagine the wonderful and
stirring scenes which form part of the play
without visualizing them. It is, I contend,
better to reserve Shakespeare for the study
than to see him presented half-heartedly.

The merely archaic presentation of the play
can be of interest only to those epicures who
do not pay their shilling to enter the theatre.
The contemporary theatre must make its
appeal to the great public, and I hold that
while one should respect every form of art,
that art which appeals only to a coterie is on
a lower plane than that which speaks to the
world. Surely, it is not too much to claim

that a truer and more vivid impression of a period of history can be given by its representation on the stage than by any other means of information. Though the archæologist with symbolic leanings may cry out, the theatre is primarily for those who love the drama, who love the joy of life and the true presentation of history. It is only secondarily for those who fulfil their souls in footnotes.*

I hold that whatever may tend to destroy the illusion and the people's understanding is to be condemned. Whatever may tend to heighten the illusion and to help the audience to a better understanding of the play and the author's meaning, is to be commended.

* FOOTNOTE.

Personally, I have been a sentimental adherent of symbolism since my first Noah's Ark. Ever since I first beheld the generous curves of Mrs. Noah, and first tasted the insidious carmine of her lips, have I regarded the wife of Noah as symbolical of the supreme type of womanhood. I have learnt that the most exclusive symbolists, when painting a meadow, regard purple as symbolical of bright green; but we live in a realistic age and have not yet overtaken the *art nouveau* of the pale future. It is difficult to deal seriously with so much earnestness. I am forced into symbolic parable. Artemus Ward, when delivering a lecture on his great moral panorama, pointed with his wand to a blur on the horizon, and said : " Ladies and gentlemen, that is a horse— the artist who painted that picture called on me yesterday with tears in his eyes, and said he would disguise that fact from me no longer ! " He, too, was a symbolist.

Henry VIII. and His Court

Shakespeare and Burbage, Betterton, Colley Cibber, the Kembles, the Keans, Phelps, Calvert and Henry Irving, as artists, recognised that there was but one way to treat the play of Henry VIII. It is pleasant to sin in such good company.

I contend that Henry VIII. is essentially a realistic and not a symbolic play. Indeed, probably no English author is less "symbolic" than Shakespeare. "Hamlet" is a play which, to my mind, does not suffer by the simplest setting; indeed, a severe simplicity of treatment seems to me to assist rather than to detract from the imaginative development of that masterpiece. But I hold that, with the exception of certain scenes in "The Tempest," no plays of Shakespeare are susceptible to what is called "symbolic" treatment. To attempt to present Henry VIII. in other than a realistic manner would be to ensure absolute failure. Let us take an instance from the text. By what symbolism can Shakespeare's stage directions in the Trial scene be represented on the stage?

"A Hall in Blackfriars. Enter two vergers with short silver wands; next them two scribes in the habit of doctors. . . . Next them with some small distance, follows a gentleman bearing the purse with the great seal and a Cardinal's hat; then two priests bearing each a silver cross; then a gentleman usher bareheaded, accompanied with a sergeant-at-arms bearing a silver mace; then two gentlemen bearing two great silver pillars; After them, side by side, the two Cardinals, Wolsey and Campeius; two noblemen with the sword and mace," etc.

I confess my symbolic imagination was completely gravelled, and in the absence of any symbolic substitute, I have been compelled to fall back on the stage directions.

Yet we are gravely told by the writer of a recent article that " all Shakespeare's plays " lend themselves of course to such symbolic treatment. We hear, indeed, that the National Theatre is to be run on symbolic lines. If it be so, then God help the National Theatre— the symbolists will not. No " ism " ever made a great cause. The National Theatre, to be the dignified memorial we all hope it may be, will owe its birth, its being and its preservation to the artists, who alone are the

guardians of any art. It is the painter, not
the frame-maker, who upholds the art of
painting ; it is the poet, not the book-binder,
who carries the torch of poetry. It was the
sculptor, and not the owner of the quarry,
who made the Venus of Milo. It is sometimes
necessary to re-assert the obvious.

Now there are plays in which symbolism
is appropriate—those of Maeterlinck, for
instance. But if, as has been said, Maeterlinck resembles Shakespeare, Shakespeare
does not resemble Maeterlinck. Let us remember that Shakespeare was a humanist,
not a symbolist.

The End

The end of the play of Henry VIII. once
more illustrates the pageantry of realism, as
prescribed in the elaborate directions as to
the christening of the new-born princess.

It is this incident of the christening of the
future Queen Elizabeth that brings to an
appropriate close the strange eventful history
as depicted in the play of Henry VIII. And
thus the injustice of the world is once more
triumphantly vindicated : Wolsey, the de-

voted servant of the King, has crept into an
ignominious sanctuary ; Katharine has been
driven to a martyr's doom ; the adulterous
union has been blessed by the Court of
Bishops ; minor poets have sung their blas-
phemous pæans in unison. The offspring of
Anne Boleyn, over whose head the Shadow
of the Axe is already hovering, has been
christened amid the acclamations of the
mob ; the King paces forth to hold the child
up to the gaze of a shouting populace, accompanied by the Court and the Clergy—
trumpets blare, drums roll, the organ thunders,
cannons boom, hymns are sung, the joy bells
are pealing.   A lonely figure in black enters
weeping.   It is the Fool !

CHRONOLOGY OF PUBLIC EVENTS DURING THE LIFETIME OF KING HENRY VIII.

1491. Birth of Henry, second son of Henry VII. and Elizabeth of York.

1501. Marriage of Arthur, Prince of Wales, eldest son of Henry VII. and Elizabeth of York, to Katharine of Aragon, daughter of Ferdinand and Isabella of Spain.

1502. Death of Arthur, Prince of Wales.

1509. Death of King Henry VII.

Marriage of Henry VIII. at Westminster Abbey with Katharine of Aragon, his brother's widow.

Thomas Wolsey made King's Almoner.

1511. Thomas Wolsey called to the King's Council.

The Holy League established by the Pope.

1512. War with France.

1513. Battles of the Spurs and of Flodden.

Wolsey becomes Chief Minister.

1516. Wolsey made Legate.

Dissolution of the Holy League.

1517. Luther denounces Indulgences.

1520. Henry meets Francis at "Field of Cloth of Gold."

Luther burns the Pope's Bull.

1521. Quarrel of Luther with Henry.

Henry VIII. and His Court

1521.   Henry's book against Luther presented to the Pope.

Pope Leo confers on Henry the title " Fidei Defensor."

1522. Renewal of war with France.

1523. Wolsey quarrels with the Commons on question of 20 per cent. property tax.

1525. Benevolences of one-tenth from the laity and of one-fourth from clergy demanded.

Exaction of Benevolences defeated.

Peace with France.

1527. Henry resolves on a Divorce.

Sack of Rome.

1528. Pope Clement VII. issues a commission to the Cardinals Wolsey and Campeggio for a trial of the facts on which Henry's application for a divorce was based.

1529. Trial of Queen Katharine at Blackfriars' Hall.

Katharine appeals to Rome.

Fall of Wolsey. Ministry of Norfolk and Sir Thomas More.

Rise of Thomas Cromwell.

1530. Wolsey arrested for treason.

Wolsey's death at Leicester Abbey.

1531. Henry acknowledged as " Supreme Head of the Church of England."

1533. Henry secretly marries Anne Boleyn.

Cranmer, in Archbishop of Canterbury's Court, declares Katharine's marriage invalid and the marriage of

Chronology of Public Events

1533. Henry and Anne lawful. Anne Boleyn crowned Queen in Westminster Abbey.

Birth of Elizabeth (Queen Elizabeth).

1535. Henry's title as Supreme Head of the Church incorporated in the royal style by letters patent.

Execution of Sir Thomas More.

1536. English Bible issued.

Dissolution of lesser Monasteries.

Death of Katharine of Aragon.

Execution of Anne Boleyn.

Henry's marriage with Jane Seymour.

1537. Birth of Edward VI.

Death of Jane Seymour.

Dissolution of greater Monasteries.

1540. Henry's marriage with Anne of Cleves.

Execution of Thomas Cromwell.

Henry divorces Anne of Cleves.

Henry's marriage with Catherine Howard.

1542. Execution of Catherine Howard.

Completion of the Tudor Conquest of Ireland.

1543. War with France.

Henry's marriage with Catherine Parr.

1547. Death of Henry. Age 55 years and 7 months. He reigned 37 years and 9 months.

SHAKESPEAREAN PLAYS PRODUCED UNDER HERBERT BEERBOHM TREE'S MANAGEMENT. A.—AT THE HAYMARKET THEATRE

1889. "The Merry Wives of Windsor."
1892. "Hamlet."
1896. "King Henry IV." (Part I.)

B.—AT HIS MAJESTY'S THEATRE

1898. " Julius Cæsar."
1899. " King John."
1900. " A Midsummer's Night's Dream."
1901. " Twelfth Night."
1903. " King Richard II."
1904. " The Tempest."
1905. " Much Ado About Nothing."
First Annual Shakespeare Festival :
" King Richard II."
" Twelfth Night."
" The Merry Wives of Windsor."
" Hamlet."
" Much Ado About Nothing."
" Julius Cæsar."
1906. " The Winter's Tale."
" Antony and Cleopatra.",
Second Annual Shakespeare Festival :
" The Tempest."

1906.   " Hamlet."
          " King Henry IV." (Part I.)
          " Julius Cæsar."
          " The Merry Wives of Windsor."

1907.   Third Annual Shakespeare Festival :
          " The Tempest."
          " The Winter's Tale."
          " Hamlet."
          " Twelfth Night."
          " Julius Cæsar."
          " The Merry Wives of Windsor."

1908.   " The Merchant of Venice."
        Fourth Annual Shakespeare Festival :
          " The Merry Wives of Windsor."
          " The Merchant of Venice."
          " Twelfth Night."
          " Hamlet."

1909.   Fifth Annual Shakespeare Festival :
          " King Richard III."
          " Twelfth Night."
          " The Merry Wives of Windsor."
          " Hamlet."
          " Julius Cæsar."
          " The Merchant of Venice."
          " Macbeth."   (Mr. Arthur Bourchier's
             Company.)
          " Antony and Cleopatra "   (Act II.,
             Scene 2).

1910.   Sixth Annual Shakespeare Festival :
          " The Merry Wives of Windsor."
          " Julius Cæsar."
          " Twelfth Night."
          " Hamlet."   (By His Majesty's Theatre

Shakespearean Plays

1910.   Company and by Mr. H. B. Irving's Company.)

" The Merchant of Venice." (By His Majesty's Theatre Company and by Mr. Arthur Bourchier's Company.)

" King Lear." (Mr. Herbert Trench's Company.)

" The Taming of the Shrew." (Mr. F. R. Benson and Company.)

" Coriolanus." (Mr. F. R. Benson and Company.)

" Two Gentlemen of Verona." (The Elizabethan Stage Society's Company.

" King Henry V." (Mr. Lewis Waller and Company.)

" King Richard II."

Scenes from " Macbeth " and " Romeo and Juliet."

1910. September 1st, " King Henry VIII."